DREAMWORKS

KUNG FU PANDA 4

PO'S GUIDE TO BEING ZEN

Andrews McMeel
PUBLISHING®

Andrews McMeel Publishing
a division of Andrews McMeel Universal
1130 Walnut Street, Kansas City, Missouri 64106

www.andrewsmcmeel.com

24 25 26 27 28 KPR 10 9 8 7 6 5 4 3 2 1

ISBN: 978-1-5248-8962-3

Editor: Erinn Pascal
Designer: Jessica Rodriguez
Production Editor: David Shaw
Production Manager: Chadd Keim

ATTENTION: SCHOOLS AND BUSINESSES

Andrews McMeel books are available at quantity discounts with bulk purchase for educational, business, or sales promotional use. For information, please e-mail the Andrews McMeel Publishing Special Sales Department: sales@amuniversal.com.

Hi! I'm Po. But you probably know me as the Dragon Warrior.

WHAT'S YOUR NAME?

_____

I'm a master of kung fu. You've probably heard of my
awesome adventures! It takes a LOT of practice,
but now I'm a master of being Zen too!

What's Zen?

Zen is a state of peace that makes you feel calm.
You know that feeling you get after eating
a REALLY good dumpling? Yeah,
it feels kind of like that.

In this book, I'll give you the SECRET
RECIPE FOR BEING ZEN. Trust me,
being Zen tastes GOOD!

WHAT MAKES YOU FEEL GOOD?

_____

_____

_____

_____

_____

_____

_____

_____

Let's do a breathing exercise now.
You might be thinking, "But Po, I already know
how to breathe!! I do it ALL THE TIME!" But
this isn't any old breathing. It's **deep breathing**.
It helps you unlock your inner Zen.

Take a deep breath in and hold it
for a moment. Master Shifu says
"inner peace" over and over again.

Then, take a deep breath out.
Kinda like an outer peace. Peace,
piece, piece of pie?

Repeat this a few times, focusing
on your inhale and exhale. You can
visualize yourself in a peaceful spot,
like at the Sacred Peach Tree
of Heavenly Wisdom.

Inner peace. Outer peace.
Inner peace. Outer peace.

Next, repeat that breathing exercise. But while you repeat it, think of something that makes you really happy. For me, that's noodles. Mmmm.

WRITE DOWN OR DRAW WHAT YOU WERE THINKING ABOUT. I'M DRAWING NOODLES. MHMMM.

_____
_____
_____
_____
_____
_____
_____
_____
_____
_____
_____
_____
_____
_____
_____
_____

Now, think of something you really want.
Maybe it's seeing everybody you love sitting at a
table with a side of steamy dumplings. Maybe it's being
someone's hero and two sides of steamy dumplings.
Y'know, I could really go for some steamy
dumplings right about now.

What do you want? Why do you want it?
What are you going to do to achieve it?

DON'T BE AFRAID. WRITE IT DOWN!

_____

_____

_____

_____

_____

_____

_____

_____

_____

_____

_____

Every kung fu master knows how important it is to practice. Sometimes that means being quiet and breathing in and out until your mind is clear and you feel calm.

The more you practice these meditations, the better you'll get at them. No one can be awesome at everything right away!

Before I became the Dragon Warrior, I wasn't all that good at kung fu. Just ask Tigress. Now look at me. *SKABLAM!*

Think about all of the times you've started . . . well, anything! Maybe it was learning kung fu. Maybe it was not giving up on something, like running up the stairs at the Jade Palace.

These things required a *lot* of practice for me.

GO AHEAD. WRITE DOWN HOW YOU STARTED—AND THEN HOW YOU PERSEVERED!

_____

_____

_____

_____

_____

_____

_____

_____

_____

_____

_____

_____

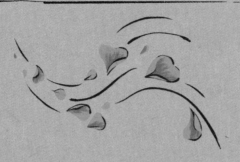

There's a tree near the Jade Palace, the
Sacred Peach Tree of Heavenly Wisdom,
where I like to sit and think.

*"Every pit holds the strength
of a mighty tree."*

We all have the potential to become more than
we are. That's what makes us awesome! It's kind of
like when I became the Dragon Warrior. Now I get
to keep growing by training my future successor,
like Master Shifu did for me.

Master Shifu is strict,
but also cool. Just don't
tell him I said that, OK?

Okay, let's do that breathing exercise again.

Inner peace. Outer peace.
Inner peace. Outer peace.

Now, think about what you can do to help others. For me, I'd like to help out my dads in the noodle restaurant more.

YOU HAVE SO MANY AWESOME TALENTS! HOW WILL YOU BECOME A MASTER?

_____

_____

_____

_____

_____

_____

_____

_____

_____

_____

_____

Have you ever heard of manifestation?

Manifestation is when you believe in yourself so much that you can make it real. Believing is the key ingredient.

My dads' noodle shop is my favorite place ever. And do you know what the secret ingredient is in his secret ingredient soup?

It's nothing! My dad *believes* the soup is good, and so it is.

Isn't that AWESOME?

"To make something special, you just have to believe it's special."

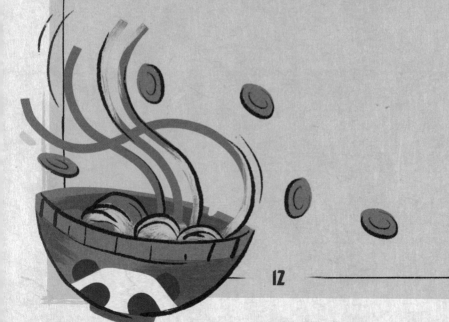

When I became the Dragon Warrior, I had to read the Dragon Scroll. It promised "limitless power," but it was actually . . . totally blank! Master Shifu insisted that the Dragon Scroll was meant to teach me something, though. And it did. The Dragon Warrior's power comes from believing in your abilities. Manifestation!

WHAT'S SOMETHING YOU REALLY WANT TO MANIFEST *TODAY?*

There's no right answer!

_____

_____

_____

_____

_____

_____

_____

_____

_____

_____

_____

_____

_____

But I can't just *want* something in order to manifest it.
I also have to make it happen. An action plan!

HOW ARE YOU GOING TO GET WHAT YOU WANT TODAY?

What's something you want to manifest by this time *next week*? Maybe there are a few somethings.

WRITE DOWN EVERYTHING YOU CAN THINK OF!

Now let's think bigger than big.

Master Shifu recently told me that I need to train a successor who will become the next Dragon Warrior after me. Then I'll be the Spiritual Leader of the Valley of Peace. I want to manifest becoming a great Spiritual Leader by coming up with cool, wise words, like *"Life's greatest enemy is—ugh, I don't know, uh, stairs?"* Okay, maybe not that, but I'm manifesting something awesome.

WHAT DO YOU WANT TO MANIFEST THIS YEAR?

_____

_____

_____

_____

_____

_____

_____

_____

_____

_____

_____

Pretend it's a year from now. What has Future You accomplished that they want to share with Present You? Write a letter.

TODAY'S DATE IS:

_____

A YEAR FROM NOW, IT WILL BE:

_____

A LETTER FROM FUTURE ME:

_____
_____
_____
_____
_____
_____
_____
_____
_____
_____
_____

_____

_____

_____

_____

_____

_____

_____

_____

_____

_____

_____

_____

_____

_____

_____

_____

This is called **visualizing**. You're putting
that manifestation into the universe!

A year from now, I'll be the Spiritual Leader of the
Valley of Peace! Expert at kung fu moves . . .
and sharing wisdom, and maybe I'll even have
a cool Spiritual Leader action figure!

I want to be the best Spiritual Leader. But that means I need to practice sharing wisdom with the Valley of Peace.

Practice is the only thing that will help me kick Spiritual Leader butt!

Now that you've started
to master manifestation, let's meditate.

Meditation is when you completely clear your mind.
Clear like an empty bowl that used to be full of noodles!
Meditation helps me find answers, like when I didn't
know who to pick as the next Dragon Warrior. Sometimes you understand best when your mind is clear.

WHAT'S A TIME THAT YOU THINK MEDITATION— CLEARING YOUR MIND—COULD'VE BEEN HELPFUL?

_____

_____

_____

_____

_____

_____

_____

_____

Go somewhere quiet and sit up straight.
Like Master Shifu, repeat:

"*Inner peace. Inner peace.*
Inner peace."

Breathe deeply, in and out.

Now, close your eyes.

Did you think of anything totally
AWESOME while meditating?

WRITE IT ALL OUT HERE.

_____
_____
_____
_____
_____
_____
_____
_____
_____
_____
_____
_____
_____
_____
_____
_____
_____
_____
_____

Meditation isn't always easy, even for the Dragon
Warrior! Sometimes I have lots of inner
Po voices in my head.

If you have a lot of inner <u>yous</u> chatting
away in your head too, it's okay. Practice
is the only way to become a master!

As Master Shifu says (and he's very wise),

*"Who you are
will always be a part of
what you become."*

I'm still learning how to share wisdom with the Valley of Peace, but I'm workshopping this quote:

"He who resorts to violence now will only find more violence later."

I shared this with a den of thieves.
I don't think they got it, but I'll meditate on it.

DO YOU HAVE A QUOTE THAT INSPIRES YOU? WHAT ARE SOME QUOTES YOU LIKE?

_____

_____

_____

_____

_____

_____

_____

_____

_____

_____

_____

_____

NOW, PICK ONE OF YOUR FAVORITE QUOTES AND DESIGN A COOL POSTER WITH IT!

I like the quote:

"Every pit holds the strength of a mighty tree."

I'm just a panda, but I also have the power of the Dragon Warrior.

WHAT DOES YOUR QUOTE MEAN TO YOU?

_____

_____

_____

_____

_____

_____

_____

_____

_____

_____

_____

Now, imagine that YOU are a very cool
and powerful hero, and you even have
YOUR OWN ACTION FIGURE!

WHAT IS YOUR SUPER COOL, WISE,
AND EPIC PROVERB? WHAT DOES YOUR
ACTION FIGURE SAY WHEN YOU POSE IT?

_____

_____

_____

_____

IF YOU NEED SOME IDEAS FOR YOUR PROVERB,
TRY THESE PROMPTS AS STARTERS. YOU MIGHT
COME UP WITH SOMETHING EPICALLY AWESOME!

A RUMBLING TUMMY IS LIKE _____

KNOWLEDGE IS _____

MASTER SHIFU IS _____

THE SOUND TREES MAKE IS LIKE _____
_____

THE PANDA WHO SLEEPS THE MOST DOES NOT ___
_____
_____

WHEN LIFE GIVES YOU PEACH PITS, _____
_____

I THINK, THEREFORE _____

FLOWERS ARE BEAUTIFUL, LIKE _____
_____

SWEET-AND-SOUR NOODLES ARE AS DELICIOUS AS

_____

DUMPLINGS TASTE LIKE _____

WISDOM IS _____

PEACE FEELS LIKE _____

KUNG FU IS COOL, BUT _____

_____ IS COOLER.

FAMILY IS _____

FRIENDS ARE _____

KICKING BUTT IS _____

THE DRAGON WARRIOR IS _____

WHAT I ADMIRE ABOUT _____ IS

_____

ASK NOT WHY THE DUMPLING IS SALTY, BUT WHY

THE SALT _____

Do you know about the five senses? They are sight, smell, sound, touch, and my favorite . . . taste.

I *see* a big bowl of noodles.

I *smell* spicy peppers in the bowl of noodles.

I *hear* the sound of spicy noodles in a bowl getting slurped.

I *touch* the spicy noodles that were in a bowl 'cuz they accidentally dribbled down my chin.

I *taste* the spicy noodles that were in a bowl 'cuz they accidentally dribbled down my chin, but I slurped them back up.

Taste is definitely my favorite sense.

RIGHT NOW, WHAT ARE YOU . . .

SEEING:

_____

_____

_____

SMELLING:

_____

_____

_____

HEARING:

_____

_____

_____

TOUCHING:

_____

_____

_____

TASTING: ← Or want to be tasting

_____

_____

_____

Another awesome way to clear your mind and meditate is to pay attention to your senses. If I'm getting kicked around in a kung fu battle, I might re-center myself by smelling my own fear. Okay, not literally, but you get the idea. Right?

ONE MORE THING I CAN SEE:

_____

_____

ONE MORE THING I CAN FEEL:

_____

_____

ONE MORE THING I CAN HEAR:

_____

_____

ONE MORE THING I CAN SMELL:

_____

_____

ONE MORE THING I CAN TASTE: ← Or want to be tasting

_____

_____

One of my favorite smells in the world is
my dad's super secret ingredient soup recipe.
Yummm. Now I'm hungry.

What's your favorite smell in the world?
What are you doing when you smell it?
Who is around you? What is around you?

WHEN YOU'RE DONE THINKING ON IT,
WRITE ALL ABOUT THAT SMELL.

_____

_____

_____

_____

_____

_____

_____

_____

_____

_____

_____

_____

Did you know that relaxing isn't just napping?
There are tons of ways you can relax. Something
that can be relaxing is doodling a pattern!

Drawing an image can be just as relaxing.

MAYBE YOU COULD DRAW ME?

Being outside is also relaxing. I like to sit
by the Sacred Peach Tree of Heavenly Wisdom.

Next time you're outside, pick a blade of grass,
a leaf, or a pebble, and paste it or rub it in
this book. Right . . . there!

Cool, huh?

When I sit by the Sacred Peach Tree of Heavenly Wisdom, I always smell peaches. I feel a gentle breeze on my face, and from time to time, I hear Master Oogway's voice in my mind.

WRITE ABOUT WHAT YOU SMELL, HEAR, OR SEE OUTSIDE.

Sometimes, when I'm out doing Dragon Warrior stuff . . . I get scared. Everyone is afraid sometimes, even me. I was terrified when Master Shifu told me that soon I'd have to pick the next Dragon Warrior. I didn't want to give it up!

Think about a time when you were afraid. You can meditate on it if you want. What would you do differently now that you've been through it? What would you do the same?

NOW, WRITE ABOUT IT BELOW!

_____

_____

_____

_____

_____

_____

_____

_____

_____

_____

_____

Change can be scary. My dad, Mr. Ping, told me that when he was younger, all he wanted was to be the greatest noodle chef in the valley. So he became the greatest noodle chef in the valley. But he *also* became a dad, and according to him, "Nothing's ever been the same since." My dad reminds me that change doesn't have to be a bad thing.

In fact, he changes the menu at his noodle restaurant constantly. If things stayed the same forever, they'd get boring!

Next time you're feeling scared, think about how you can overcome it.

My other dad, Li, also experienced change. He left his panda village and moved to the Valley of Peace. Now, he chases after me on Dragon Warrior missions! Isn't that awesome?

When was a time that you experienced change? How did you handle it? What would you like to do differently next time you have a change?

THINK ABOUT IT, THEN WRITE YOUR ANSWERS BELOW!

_____

_____

_____

_____

_____

_____

_____

_____

_____

_____

Yoga is a super awesome ancient practice combining physical poses, mindfulness, and breathing exercises all together.

Yoga can help you feel WAY more Zen.

Plus, yoga poses always have super cool names, just like the poses in kung fu!

MOUNTAIN POSE

This pose is called **Mountain Pose**.

Imagine that there's this really cool artist in town, and she's drawing a portrait of you that's going to be displayed in the Jade Palace. To get the best picture, you have to stand really still and totally straight, like there's a line from the top of your head to the bottom of your toes.

Next you'll want to slide your shoulders back and put most of your weight on your heels.

This is a perfectly aligned **Mountain Pose!**

DOWNWARD PANDA

Now, let's try another yoga pose. This one is called
Downward Dog. Don't ask me why it's called that.
I call it Downward Panda.

STEP 1: On a soft surface, get on your hands and knees.

STEP 2: Push back through your hands to lift your hips
off the ground. Keep your legs straight as you do this.
Spread out your fingers if it helps you balance. (**Po Tip**,
which is kind of like **_pro tip_**: Your head should hang
kinda comfortably between your hands, and your
shoulders should not touch your ears.)

STEP 3: Another **Po Tip**: Keep your butt up high! Your heels should touch the ground.

STEP 4: Okay, you're almost done! Now exhale, bend your knees, and come out of the position!

STEP 5: You've mastered Downward *Panda*! You may not get this yoga pose right on the first try. But keep practicing! (Trust me, it took a lot of practice for me to become the Dragon Warrior!)

DRAGON WARRIOR II

OK, technically it's called **Warrior II**, but it's **Dragon Warrior II** when I'm doing it!

STEP I: We start in Mountain Pose.

STEP 2: Next, step your feet apart and stretch your arms out wide with your hands facing down.

STEP 3: Turn one foot so that it points to the side. Then bend that knee.

STEP 4: Now here's that big moment! Look at your hand that's extended above the pointed leg. Now, hold the pose and stretch for a few moments. When it feels good, switch sides.

STEP 5: You've mastered **Dragon Warrior II!**

Even though I'm the Dragon Warrior, I still need to encourage myself to be awesome!

My favorite affirmation is

"I am the Dragon Warrior!"

WHAT ARE SOME AFFIRMATIONS YOU'D LIKE TO USE? WRITE THEM DOWN BELOW!

_____

_____

_____

_____

_____

_____

_____

_____

PEACH TREE OF HEAVENLY WISDOM POSE

I like to picture the Sacred Peach Tree
of Heavenly Wisdom here.

STEP 1: Start in Mountain Pose again.

STEP 2: Bend one of your knees outward and rest your
foot on the other knee. (**Po Tip:** If that's too tricky, lift
your foot as high as you can. Bendy poses really
do require practice. . . .)

STEP 3: Now stretch your arms
high up over your head and put them together.

STEP 4: Big pose moment time! Hold the pose and stretch for a few moments. Looks awesome, huh?

STEP 5: Now you've mastered Peach Tree of Heavenly Wisdom pose!

JOURNAL TIME!!! WHAT DOES KINDNESS MEAN TO YOU?

_____

_____

_____

_____

_____

_____

_____

_____

_____

_____

_____

_____

_____

Another big part of being Zen is learning how to forgive. It was really hard to forgive Zhen after she cheated during a game of mahjong, but here's some sage panda wisdom:

It's never too late to do the right thing.

CAN YOU THINK OF A TIME WHEN YOU DID SOMETHING WRONG? HOW DID YOU APOLOGIZE? DID YOU END UP DOING THE RIGHT THING?

_____

_____

_____

_____

_____

_____

_____

What about a time when someone apologized to you?

HOW'D IT FEEL TO BE ON THE OTHER
SIDE OF THINGS?

_____

_____

_____

_____

_____

_____

_____

_____

_____

_____

_____

_____

_____

_____

_____

_____

_____

_____

_____

Choosing to let go and forgive others is
one of the most mindful and Zen things you can do.

Whoa. That was pretty good wisdom, huh? I think
I'm getting better at this Spiritual Leader stuff!

WHAT'S THE SITUATION—
WHAT WOULD YOU LIKE TO MOVE ON FROM?
For me, Zhen got us into a bit of trouble when she cheated while playing a game of mahjong.

OOH, TELL ME MORE.
WHAT HAPPENED? WHY WAS IT UNFAIR?
While Zhen and I were trying to find out how to get to Juniper City, we entered a tavern. I tried to get us help, but Zhen decided to play a game of mahjong . . . and kept all of the game pieces hidden in her tail. She then made everyone at the tavern mad at her, including me!

WHAT HAPPENS IF YOU
FORGIVE WHAT HAPPENED?
We get to continue our journey together.

AND WHAT HAPPENS IF YOU DON'T?
I'll have to go to Juniper City alone . . . and Zhen and I won't get to go on an adventure together!

To understand Zhen, I had to think as if I WAS her. This is called **empathy**. Zhen likes winning. She wasn't trying to make me mad on purpose.

Wanna try an an empathy activity?

**IMAGINE YOU'RE MASTER SHIFU.
WHAT DO YOU THINK HE'S FEELING?
WHAT DO YOU THINK HE'S THINKING?**

_____

_____

_____

_____

_____

_____

_____

_____

_____

_____

_____

_____

_____

I really wish I'd had a map to Juniper City—honestly, it would've made my travels with Zhen SO MUCH EASIER. Did you know that you can make maps of EMPATHY too? Think about someone in your life and something that happened to them recently.

DRAW A PHOTO OF THEM BELOW, AND THEN WRITE OR DRAW WHAT YOU THINK THEY'RE . . .

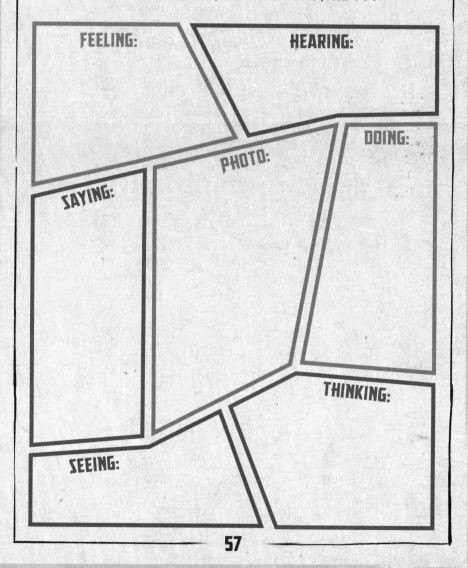

FEELING:

HEARING:

DOING:

PHOTO:

SAYING:

THINKING:

SEEING:

I was late to the grand opening of my dads' noodle restaurant. Next time, I can make sure to be on time. I can also tell them I'm sorry.

WHAT IS SOMETHING YOU CAN DO FOR YOUR PERSON?

_____

_____

_____

_____

_____

_____

_____

_____

_____

_____

_____

_____

_____

_____

To master being Zen, you have to
practice gratitude too.

I'm thankful for my dads, Master Shifu,
Zhen, noodles and dumplings, and getting
to be the Dragon Warrior.

WHAT ARE YOU THANKFUL FOR?

_____
_____
_____
_____
_____
_____
_____
_____
_____
_____
_____
_____

Soon I'll start a new role as Spiritual Leader of the Valley of Peace, where I'll help others and teach them how to be Zen.

Who knows where this journey will take me—all I know is that it's time to kick some Spiritual Leader butt. I'm manifesting being the best Spiritual Leader EVER right now.

Oh, and remember that SECRET RECIPE I promised you? Well, the secret recipe is all your own. Kinda like my dad's. The secret ingredient soup recipe to being Zen is up to you!

It's time to discover some wisdom all on your own!
How will you become a Zen master? Journal it out
and discover your own AWESOME!!!

Happy
Journaling!!!